The lush green folds of Nāpali tell an ancient story etched by lava, rains, and time.

*Lumaha'i is a study in dramatic contrasts—
flamboyant pinks flirt with shocking greens . . .*

. . . stark black lava floats in a cool blue ocean.

Timeless trails of rainwater have transformed the Kalalau Valley into staggering cathedral spires.

(At left) Suspended over sand and sea, the remote Kalalau Trail ends where another world begins.

A late-day sun glows golden on the shores of Hā'ena Beach.

Perched at the water's edge, the thirteenth hole at Kiele Course, Kaua'i Lagoons, basks in the afternoon light.

A masterful portrait comes to life in searing shades of scarlet; a band of lacy white streaks the canyon walls.

(At right) "The Grand Canyon of the Pacific," Waimea Canyon, explodes in infinite detail.

Dusk chases a setting sun at Polihale Beach, the tiny islands of Niʻihau and Lehua in the distance.

Below luxurious Princeville Resort, Puʻupōā Beach presents an oasis of calm.

Rooted deeply in the wisdom of generations, Kauaʻi's people live their ancient culture.

(At left) A flush of sea spray meets a coral sky at "the end of the road," offshore from Kēʻē Beach.

Only accessible by foot, ocean, or air, the Kalalau Valley inspires silent reverence . . .

. . . just beyond, the rugged knuckles of the pali touch the sea.

The westernmost point of the island, the striking sandscape of Polihale Beach blazes in the setting sun.

Within the Hanalei Valley, patches, or loʻi, of revered Hawaiian taro, grow in standing water like rice.

(At left) From above, the quilted Hanalei Valley unfurls in a spectrum of green.

Kaua'i's ceaseless abundance gushes over twin Wailua Falls.

Through a west-side lava outcrop, a joyous spectacle known as "the Spouting Horn" erupts.

From an overlook in high Kōke'e, the Kalalau Valley stretches toward a seamless blue horizon.

As twilight approaches, a veil of misty cloud cover brushes Kalalau's face.

Kaua'i's affinity for purple appears everywhere—in lei strung across a pā'ū rider's shoulders; overflowing from the bed of an abandoned truck; in the delicate yet racy blooms of the bougainvillea.

A lone sentinel of the North Shore, Kilauea Lighthouse keeps watch over a brilliant blue Pacific.

Nāwiliwili Bay and Harbor claim most visitors' first glimpse of the Garden Island.

Cushioned deep within a moist interior, Mānāwaipuna Falls remains a secluded secret.

Literally dripping with life, Fern Grotto beckons with its feathery green embrace.

Weathering the annals of time, Alekoko Fishpond (or Menehune Fishpond) and the sacred burial grounds of Kaulupaoa Heiau stand testament to Hawai'i's vital heritage.

(At right) The Wailua River lays a curving blue ribbon through the emerald landscape.

Immortalized in the memorable South Pacific, "Bali Hai" grows florid against a ruby sky.